THIS BOOK BELONGS TO

_____

START DATE

_____

SHE READS TRUTH

EXECUTIVE

FOUNDER/CHIEF EXECUTIVE OFFICER
Raechel Myers

CO-FOUNDER/CHIEF CONTENT OFFICER
Amanda Bible Williams

CHIEF OPERATING OFFICER
Ryan Myers

EDITORIAL

CONTENT DIRECTOR
Jessica Lamb

DIGITAL MANAGING EDITOR
Oghosa Iyamu, MDiv

PRODUCTION EDITOR
Hannah Little, MTS

MARKETING CONTENT EDITOR
Tameshia Williams, ThM

ASSOCIATE EDITOR
Lindsey Jacobi, MDiv

MARKETING

MARKETING DIRECTOR
Kamron Kunce

GROWTH MARKETING MANAGER
Blake Showalter

PRODUCT MARKETING MANAGER
Megan Phillips

SOCIAL MEDIA STRATEGIST
Taylor Krupp

CREATIVE

CREATIVE DIRECTOR
Amy Dennis

DESIGN MANAGER
Kelsea Allen

ART DIRECTOR
Aimee Lindamood

DESIGNERS
Abbey Benson
Amanda Brush, MA
Annie Glover
Lauren Haag

JUNIOR DESIGNER
Jessie Gerakinis

OPERATIONS

OPERATIONS DIRECTOR
Allison Sutton

OFFICE MANAGER
Nicole Quirion

PROJECT ASSISTANT
Mary Beth Montgomery

SHIPPING

SHIPPING MANAGER
Marian Byne

FULFILLMENT LEAD
Cait Baggerman

FULFILLMENT SPECIALISTS
Kajsa Matheny
Noe Sanchez

SUBSCRIPTION INQUIRIES
orders@shereadstruth.com

COMMUNITY SUPPORT

COMMUNITY EXPERIENCE DIRECTOR
Kara Hewett, MOL

COMMUNITY SUPPORT SPECIALISTS
Katy McKnight
Heather Vollono
Margot Williams

CONTRIBUTORS

SPECIAL THANKS
Beth Joseph
Taura Ryan
Logan Click

@SHEREADSTRUTH

Download the She Reads Truth app, available for iOS and Android

Subscribe to the
She Reads Truth podcast

This book was printed offset in Nashville, Tennessee, on 70# Lynx Opaque. Cover is 100# Cougar Opaque with a soft touch lamination.

A LIVING HOPE

A BIBLICAL STUDY OF RESURRECTED LIFE IN CHRIST

SHE READS TRUTH

Jesus invites us
to share in His
resurrected life.

Raechel Myers
FOUNDER/CHIEF
EXECUTIVE OFFICER

L ast year, in the final days of winter, the beloved patriarch of our family died. We gathered a few days later to lay his body in the ground. It was the second day of spring.

The Bible offers words of comfort about what happens to believers when they die—promises of eternal life secured by Jesus's own life, death, and resurrection. I know these words are true in every season, but standing at my grandpa's graveside that day, the significance of the timing brought a special kind of solace. At the church I reminded Grandpa's family and friends of Paul's words from 1 Corinthians 15: Our earthly bodies are but seeds of what our heavenly bodies will become. "What you sow does not come to life unless it dies," and we "are not sowing the body that will be, but only a seed" (vv. 36–37).

Grandpa died in winter, and we were burying his body at the beginning of spring, like a seed of promise planted in the ground. The act of placing a body in the ground was an act of faith and defiance, declaring, "This is not the end. This is only the beginning." Because of Jesus, the resting place of every believer is the site of a future resurrection.

Jesus, the firstfruits from among the dead, invites us to share in His resurrected life (1 Corinthians 15:20). His resurrection both shapes and secures our hope—not only in death, but also right now, in this life! "Because of his great mercy he has given us new birth into a living hope through the resurrection of Jesus Christ from the dead and into an inheritance that is imperishable, undefiled, and unfading, kept in heaven for you" (1 Peter 1:3b–4). Christ's resurrection changes how we understand death, but it also changes how we view life in Christ even now.

Over the next three weeks, we'll take a closer look at Jesus's life from the time of His resurrection to His ascension, reading about the encounters He had with His disciples and others after He was raised from the dead. We'll look to Scripture to learn how Christ's resurrection changes everything for those who put their faith in Him. As you walk through this Study Book, allow the daily response questions to help you process what you're observing and learning in Scripture. Don't miss the other study tools you'll find along the way, like the "Hope Even in Death" extra on page 93 (so many powerful passages in one place!). May the truth of God's Word capture your heart with the reality of the resurrected Jesus. He is our living hope.

Design on Purpose

For this Study Book design, our team created and photographed a custom art installation inspired by stained glass as a reminder of the beauty and glory of the resurrected life we find in Christ. Stained glass comes to life when light shines through it, like the living hope believers are invited into because of Christ's resurrection. You'll also see custom stained glass illustrations inspired by the art-deco style. Utilizing bright, celebratory colors, every stained glass element is a reminder that even when things feel dark or broken, our resurrected Christ is still restoring all things to life.

HOW TO USE THIS BOOK

She Reads Truth is a community of women dedicated to reading the Word of God every day. In this **A Living Hope** reading plan, we will read the accounts of Jesus's post-resurrection appearances and explore what Scripture says about how the resurrection shapes both the present and future for believers.

READ & REFLECT

Your **A Living Hope** Study Book focuses primarily on Scripture, with added features to come alongside your time with God's Word.

SCRIPTURE READING

Designed for a Monday start, this Study Book presents daily readings on Christ's resurrection and what it means for believers.

◗ *Additional passages are marked in your daily reading with the Going Deeper heading.*

REFLECTION

Each weekday features questions and space for personal reflection.

COMMUNITY & CONVERSATION

You can start reading this book at any time! If you want to join women from Sacramento to Slovenia as they read along with you, the She Reads Truth community will start Day 1 of **A Living Hope** on Monday, April 10, 2023.

 ### SHE READS TRUTH APP

Devotionals corresponding to each daily reading can be found in the **A Living Hope** reading plan on the She Reads Truth app. New devotionals will be published each weekday once the plan begins on Monday, April 10, 2023. You can use the app to participate in community discussion and more.

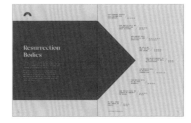

GRACE DAY

Use Saturdays to catch up on your reading, pray, and rest in the presence of the Lord.

WEEKLY TRUTH

Sundays are set aside for Scripture memorization.

See tips for memorizing Scripture on page 116.

EXTRAS

This book features additional tools to help you gain a deeper understanding of the text.

Find a complete list of extras on page 10.

 SHEREADSTRUTH.COM

The **A Living Hope** reading plan and devotionals will also be available at SheReadsTruth.com as the community reads each day. Invite your family, friends, and neighbors to read along with you!

 SHE READS TRUTH PODCAST

Subscribe to the She Reads Truth podcast and join our founders and their guests each week as they talk about what you'll read in the week ahead.

 Podcast episodes 175–177 for our **A Living Hope** *series release on Mondays beginning April 10, 2023.*

Table of Contents

SECTION TWO

Blessed be the God and Father of our Lord Jesus Christ. Because of his great mercy he has given us new birth into a living hope through the resurrection of Jesus Christ from the dead and into an inheritance that is imperishable, undefiled, and unfading, kept in heaven for you.

1 PETER 1:3-4

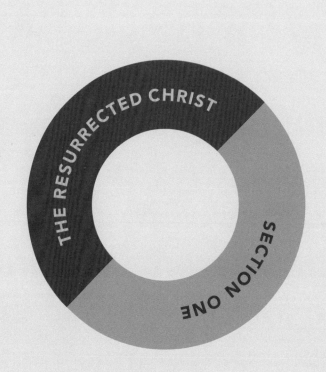

THE RESURRECTED CHRIST

SECTION ONE

In this first week, we'll read various encounters Jesus had with His followers in the days and weeks after His resurrection. Each day includes a margin note indicating when Jesus's appearance occurred.

SECTION ONE

The Women See the Resurrected Christ

I have seen the Lord!

JOHN 20:18

MATTHEW 27:57-66

The Burial of Jesus

⁵⁷ When it was evening, a rich man from Arimathea named Joseph came, who himself had also become a disciple of Jesus. ⁵⁸ He approached Pilate and asked for Jesus's body. Then Pilate ordered that it be released. ⁵⁹ So Joseph took the body, wrapped it in clean, fine linen, ⁶⁰ and placed it in his new tomb, which he had cut into the rock. He left after rolling a great stone against the entrance of the tomb. ⁶¹ Mary Magdalene and the other Mary were seated there, facing the tomb.

The Closely Guarded Tomb

⁶² The next day, which followed the preparation day, the chief priests and the Pharisees gathered before Pilate ⁶³ and said, "Sir, we remember that while this deceiver was still alive he said, 'After three days I will rise again.' ⁶⁴ So give orders that the tomb be made secure until the third day. Otherwise, his disciples may come, steal him, and tell the people, 'He has been raised from the dead,' and the last deception will be worse than the first."

⁶⁵ "Take guards," Pilate told them. "Go and make it as secure as you know how." ⁶⁶ They went and secured the tomb by setting a seal on the stone and placing the guards.

MARK 16:1-7

Resurrection Morning

¹ When the Sabbath was over, Mary Magdalene, Mary the mother of James, and Salome bought spices, so that they could go and anoint him. ² Very early in the morning, on the first day of the week, they went to the tomb at sunrise. ³ They were saying to one another, "Who will roll away the stone from the entrance to the tomb for us?" ⁴ Looking up, they noticed that the stone—which was very large—had been rolled away.

⁵ When they entered the tomb, they saw a young man dressed in a white robe sitting on the right side; they were alarmed. ⁶ "Don't be alarmed," he told them. "You are looking for Jesus of Nazareth, who was crucified. He has risen! He is not here. See the place where they put him. ⁷ But go, tell his disciples and Peter, 'He is going ahead of you to Galilee; you will see him there just as he told you.'"

JOHN 20:1-18

The Empty Tomb

¹ On the first day of the week Mary Magdalene came to the tomb early, while it was still dark. She saw that the stone had been removed from the tomb. ² So she went running to Simon Peter and to the other disciple, the one Jesus loved, and said to them, "They've taken the Lord out of the tomb, and we don't know where they've put him!"

³ At that, Peter and the other disciple went out, heading for the tomb. ⁴ The two were running together, but the other disciple outran Peter and got to the tomb first. ⁵ Stooping down, he saw the linen cloths lying there, but he did not go in. ⁶ Then, following him, Simon Peter also came. He entered the tomb and saw the linen cloths lying there. ⁷ The wrapping that had been on his head was not lying with the linen cloths but was folded up in a separate place by itself. ⁸ The other disciple, who had reached the tomb first, then also went in, saw, and believed. ⁹ For they did not yet understand the Scripture that he must rise from the dead. ¹⁰ Then the disciples returned to the place where they were staying.

Mary Magdalene Sees the Risen Lord

¹¹ But Mary stood outside the tomb, crying. As she was crying, she stooped to look into the tomb. ¹² She saw two

angels in white sitting where Jesus's body had been lying, one at the head and the other at the feet. ¹³ They said to her, "Woman, why are you crying?"

"Because they've taken away my Lord," she told them, "and I don't know where they've put him."

¹⁴ Having said this, she turned around and saw Jesus standing there, but she did not know it was Jesus. ¹⁵ "Woman," Jesus said to her, "why are you crying? Who is it that you're seeking?"

Supposing he was the gardener, she replied, "Sir, if you've carried him away, tell me where you've put him, and I will take him away."

¹⁶ Jesus said to her, "Mary."

Turning around, she said to him in Aramaic, "*Rabboni!*"—which means "Teacher."

¹⁷ "Don't cling to me," Jesus told her, "since I have not yet ascended to the Father. But go to my brothers and tell them that I am ascending to my Father and your Father, to my God and your God."

¹⁸ Mary Magdalene went and announced to the disciples, "I have seen the Lord!" And she told them what he had said to her.

◗ GOING DEEPER

ISAIAH 53

¹ Who has believed what we have heard?
And to whom has the arm of the LORD been revealed?
² He grew up before him like a young plant
and like a root out of dry ground.
He didn't have an impressive form
or majesty that we should look at him,
no appearance that we should desire him.
³ He was despised and rejected by men,
a man of suffering who knew what sickness was.
He was like someone people turned away from;
he was despised, and we didn't value him.

⁴ Yet he himself bore our sicknesses,
and he carried our pains;
but we in turn regarded him stricken,
struck down by God, and afflicted.
⁵ But he was pierced because of our rebellion,
crushed because of our iniquities;
punishment for our peace was on him,
and we are healed by his wounds.
⁶ We all went astray like sheep;
we all have turned to our own way;
and the LORD has punished him
for the iniquity of us all.

⁷ He was oppressed and afflicted,
yet he did not open his mouth.
Like a lamb led to the slaughter
and like a sheep silent before her shearers,
he did not open his mouth.
⁸ He was taken away because of oppression and judgment,
and who considered his fate?
For he was cut off from the land of the living;
he was struck because of my people's rebellion.
⁹ He was assigned a grave with the wicked,
but he was with a rich man at his death,
because he had done no violence
and had not spoken deceitfully.

¹⁰ Yet the LORD was pleased to crush him severely.
When you make him a guilt offering,
he will see his seed, he will prolong his days,
and by his hand, the LORD's pleasure will be accomplished.
¹¹ After his anguish,
he will see light and be satisfied.
By his knowledge,
my righteous servant will justify many,
and he will carry their iniquities.
¹² Therefore I will give him the many as a portion,
and he will receive the mighty as spoil,
because he willingly submitted to death,
and was counted among the rebels;
yet he bore the sin of many
and interceded for the rebels.

DATE: /   /

WHAT WAS THE RESPONSE OF THOSE WHO FIRST LEARNED OF CHRIST'S RESURRECTION?

HOW WILL I RESPOND TO THE ONGOING TRUTH OF CHRIST'S RESURRECTION TODAY?

The Resurrected Christ on the Emmaus Road

Then their eyes were opened, and they recognized him...

LUKE 24:31

LUKE 24:13–32

The Emmaus Disciples

[13] Now that same day two of them were on their way to a village called Emmaus, which was about seven miles from Jerusalem. [14] Together they were discussing everything that had taken place. [15] And while they were discussing and arguing, Jesus himself came near and began to walk along with them. [16] But they were prevented from recognizing him. [17] Then he asked them, "What is this dispute that you're having with each other as you are walking?" And they stopped walking and looked discouraged.

[18] The one named Cleopas answered him, "Are you the only visitor in Jerusalem who doesn't know the things that happened there in these days?"

[19] "What things?" he asked them.

So they said to him, "The things concerning Jesus of Nazareth, who was a prophet powerful in action and speech before God and all the people, [20] and how our chief priests and leaders handed him over to be sentenced to death, and they crucified him. [21] But we were hoping that he was the one who was about to redeem Israel. Besides all this, it's the third day since these things happened. [22] Moreover, some women from our group astounded us. They arrived early at the tomb, [23] and when they didn't find his body, they came and reported that they had seen a vision of angels who said he was alive. [24] Some of those who were with us went to the tomb and found it just as the women had said, but they didn't see him."

²⁵ He said to them, "How foolish you are, and how slow to believe all that the prophets have spoken! ²⁶ Wasn't it necessary for the Messiah to suffer these things and enter into his glory?" ²⁷ Then beginning with Moses and all the Prophets, he interpreted for them the things concerning himself in all the Scriptures.

²⁸ They came near the village where they were going, and he gave the impression that he was going farther. ²⁹ But they urged him, "Stay with us, because it's almost evening, and now the day is almost over." So he went in to stay with them.

³⁰ It was as he reclined at the table with them that he took the bread, blessed and broke it, and gave it to them. ³¹ Then their eyes were opened, and they recognized him, but he disappeared from their sight. ³² They said to each other, "Weren't our hearts burning within us while he was talking with us on the road and explaining the Scriptures to us?"

◆ GOING DEEPER

ACTS 13:16–38

¹⁶ Paul stood up and motioned with his hand and said, "Fellow Israelites, and you who fear God, listen! ¹⁷ The God of this people Israel chose our ancestors, made the people prosper during their stay in the land of Egypt, and led them out of it with a mighty arm. ¹⁸ And for about forty years he put up with them in the wilderness; ¹⁹ and after destroying seven nations in the land of Canaan, he gave them their land as an inheritance. ²⁰ This all took about 450 years. After this, he gave them judges until Samuel the prophet. ²¹ Then they asked for a king, and God gave them Saul the son of Kish, a man of the tribe of Benjamin, for forty years. ²² After removing him, he raised up David as their king and testified about him, 'I have found David the son of Jesse to be a man after my own heart, who will carry out all my will.'

²³ "From this man's descendants, as he promised, God brought to Israel the Savior, Jesus. ²⁴ Before his coming to public attention, John had previously proclaimed a baptism of repentance to all the people of Israel. ²⁵ Now as John was completing his mission, he said, 'Who do you think I am? I am not the one. But one is coming after me, and I am not worthy to untie the sandals on his feet.'

²⁶ "Brothers and sisters, children of Abraham's race, and those among you who fear God, it is to us that the word of this salvation has been sent. ²⁷ Since the residents of Jerusalem and their rulers did not recognize him or the sayings of the prophets that are read every Sabbath, they have fulfilled their words by condemning him. ²⁸ Though they found no grounds for the death sentence, they asked Pilate to have him killed. ²⁹ When they had carried out all that had been written about him, they took him down from the tree and put him in a tomb.

³⁰ But God raised him from the dead,
³¹ and he appeared for many days
to those who came up with him from
Galilee to Jerusalem,

who are now his witnesses to the people. ³² And we ourselves proclaim to you the good news of the promise that was made to our ancestors. ³³ God has fulfilled this for us, their children, by raising up Jesus, as it is written in the second Psalm:

You are my Son;
today I have become your Father.

³⁴ As to his raising him from the dead, never to return to decay, he has spoken in this way, I will give you the holy and sure promises of David. ³⁵ Therefore he also says in another passage, You will not let your Holy One see decay. ³⁶ For David, after serving God's purpose in his own generation, fell asleep, was buried with his fathers, and decayed, ³⁷ but the one God raised up did not decay. ³⁸ Therefore, let it be known to you, brothers and sisters, that through this man forgiveness of sins is being proclaimed to you."

DATE: /   /

HOW DID THE TWO DISCIPLES RESPOND TO THE RESURRECTED CHRIST?

HOW DOES JESUS'S RESPONSE TO THE TWO DISCIPLES COMFORT ME AS I SEEK TO UNDERSTAND HIS WORD TODAY?

"

Easter was when Hope in person surprised
the whole world by coming forward from the
future into the present.

N. T. WRIGHT

The Disciples See the Resurrected Christ

"Don't be faithless, but believe."

JOHN 20:27

LUKE 24:33–49

³³ That very hour they got up and returned to Jerusalem. They found the Eleven and those with them gathered together, ³⁴ who said, "The Lord has truly been raised and has appeared to Simon!" ³⁵ Then they began to describe what had happened on the road and how he was made known to them in the breaking of the bread.

The Reality of the Risen Jesus

³⁶ As they were saying these things, he himself stood in their midst. He said to them, "Peace to you!" ³⁷ But they were startled and terrified and thought they were seeing a ghost. ³⁸ "Why are you troubled?" he asked them. "And why do doubts arise in your hearts? ³⁹ Look at my hands and my feet, that it is I myself! Touch me and see, because a ghost does not have flesh and bones as you can see I have." ⁴⁰ Having said this, he showed them his hands and feet. ⁴¹ But while they still were amazed and in disbelief because of their joy, he asked them, "Do you have anything here to eat?" ⁴² So they gave him a piece of a broiled fish, ⁴³ and he took it and ate in their presence.

⁴⁴ He told them, "These are my words that I spoke to you while I was still with you—that everything written about me in the Law of Moses,

the Prophets, and the Psalms must be fulfilled." [45] Then he opened their minds to understand the Scriptures. [46] He also said to them, "This is what is written: The Messiah will suffer and rise from the dead the third day, [47] and repentance for forgiveness of sins will be proclaimed in his name to all the nations, beginning at Jerusalem. [48] You are witnesses of these things. [49] And look, I am sending you what my Father promised. As for you, stay in the city until you are empowered from on high."

JOHN 20:24–28

Thomas Sees and Believes

[24] But Thomas (called "Twin"), one of the Twelve, was not with them when Jesus came. [25] So the other disciples were telling him, "We've seen the Lord!"

But he said to them, "If I don't see the mark of the nails in his hands, put my finger into the mark of the nails, and put my hand into his side, I will never believe."

[26] A week later his disciples were indoors again, and Thomas was with them. Even though the doors were locked, Jesus came and stood among them and said, "Peace be with you."

[27] Then he said to Thomas, "Put your finger here and look at my hands. Reach out your hand and put it into my side. Don't be faithless, but believe."

[28] Thomas responded to him, "My Lord and my God!"

♥ GOING DEEPER

1 PETER 1:3–12

A Living Hope

[3] Blessed be the God and Father of our Lord Jesus Christ. Because of his great mercy he has given us new birth into a living hope through the resurrection of Jesus Christ from the dead [4] and into an inheritance that is imperishable, undefiled, and unfading, kept in heaven for you. [5] You are being guarded by God's power through faith for a salvation that is ready to be revealed in the last time. [6] You rejoice in this, even though now for a short time, if necessary, you suffer grief in various trials [7] so that the proven character of your faith—more valuable than gold which, though perishable, is refined by fire—may result in praise, glory, and honor at the revelation of Jesus Christ. [8] Though you have not seen him, you love him; though not seeing him now, you believe in him, and you rejoice with inexpressible and glorious joy, [9] because you are receiving the goal of your faith, the salvation of your souls.

[10] Concerning this salvation, the prophets, who prophesied about the grace that would come to you, searched and carefully investigated. [11] They inquired into what time or what circumstances the Spirit of Christ within them was indicating when he testified in advance to the sufferings of Christ and the glories that would follow. [12] It was revealed to them that they were not serving themselves but you. These things have now been announced to you through those who preached the gospel to you by the Holy Spirit sent from heaven—angels long to catch a glimpse of these things.

DATE: /   /

WHAT WERE THE DISCIPLES' AND THOMAS'S RESPONSES TO THE RESURRECTED CHRIST?

WHAT DOUBTS OR MISUNDERSTANDINGS KEEP ME FROM EMBRACING THE RESURRECTED CHRIST?

Resurrection Bodies

Because Christ has conquered death, eternity for the believer is secure. In the new heavens and new earth, all things are made new. This includes both creation and our physical bodies.

When Christ returns, believers will share in Jesus's resurrection (1Co 15:20-23). We also will receive restored bodies (1Co 15:47-49). What we will be has not yet been fully revealed (1Jn 3:2), but here is what Scripture does say about our future state.

OUR CURRENT BODIES
WILL BECOME OUR
NEW BODIES.   1CO 15:35-38

OUR BODIES WILL BE
TRANSFORMED AND
MADE GLORIOUS.   1CO 15:51-52;
                          PHP 3:21

OUR BODIES WILL
BE PHYSICAL AND
SPIRITUAL.   MT 28:9; JN 20:27;
                       1CO 15:42-44

WE WILL BE
ABLE TO EAT
AND DRINK.   LK 24:41-43;
                     JN 21:12-13

OUR RELATIONSHIP TO
TIME AND SPACE WILL
BE DIFFERENT.   LK 24:31;
                        JN 20:19

OUR BODIES WILL
BE WITHOUT
CORRUPTION.   1CO 15:42, 52

OUR BODIES WILL
BE WITHOUT
WEAKNESS.   1CO 15:42-43

OUR BODIES WILL NO
LONGER BE SUBJECT
TO DEATH.   1CO 15:54-55;
                       RV 21:4

WE WILL BEAR
THE IMAGE OF
CHRIST.   1CO 15:49;
                   1JN 3:2

Peter's Restoration to the Resurrected Christ

...he told him, "Follow me."

JOHN 21:19

JOHN 21:1–23

Jesus's Third Appearance to the Disciples

¹ After this, Jesus revealed himself again to his disciples by the Sea of Tiberias. He revealed himself in this way:

² Simon Peter, Thomas (called "Twin"), Nathanael from Cana of Galilee, Zebedee's sons, and two others of his disciples were together.

³ "I'm going fishing," Simon Peter said to them.

"We're coming with you," they told him. They went out and got into the boat, but that night they caught nothing.

⁴ When daybreak came, Jesus stood on the shore, but the disciples did not know it was Jesus. ⁵ "Friends," Jesus called to them, "you don't have any fish, do you?"

"No," they answered.

⁶ "Cast the net on the right side of the boat," he told them, "and you'll find some." So they did, and they were unable to haul it in because of the large number of fish. ⁷ The disciple, the one Jesus loved, said to Peter, "It is the Lord!"

When Simon Peter heard that it was the Lord, he tied his outer clothing around him (for he had taken it off) and plunged into the sea. ⁸ Since they were not far from land (about a hundred yards away), the other disciples came in the boat, dragging the net full of fish.

⁹ When they got out on land, they saw a charcoal fire there, with fish lying on it, and bread. ¹⁰ "Bring some of the fish you've just caught," Jesus told them. ¹¹ So Simon Peter climbed up and hauled the net ashore, full of large fish—153 of them. Even though there were so many, the net was not torn.

¹² "Come and have breakfast," Jesus told them.

None of the disciples dared ask him, "Who are you?" because they knew it was the Lord.

¹³ Jesus came, took the bread, and gave it to them. He did the same with the fish. ¹⁴ This was now the third time Jesus appeared to the disciples after he was raised from the dead.

Jesus's Threefold Restoration of Peter

¹⁵ When they had eaten breakfast, Jesus asked Simon Peter, "Simon, son of John, do you love me more than these?"

"Yes, Lord," he said to him, "you know that I love you."

"Feed my lambs," he told him. ¹⁶ A second time he asked him, "Simon, son of John, do you love me?"

"Yes, Lord," he said to him, "you know that I love you."

"Shepherd my sheep," he told him.

¹⁷ He asked him the third time, "Simon, son of John, do you love me?"

Peter was grieved that he asked him the third time, "Do you love me?" He said, "Lord, you know everything; you know that I love you."

"Feed my sheep," Jesus said. ¹⁸ "Truly I tell you, when you were younger, you would tie your belt and walk wherever you wanted. But when you grow old, you will stretch out your hands and someone else will tie you and carry you where you don't want to go." ¹⁹ He said this to indicate by what kind of death Peter would glorify God. After saying this, he told him, "Follow me."

Correcting a False Report

²⁰ So Peter turned around and saw the disciple Jesus loved following them, the one who had leaned back against Jesus at the supper and asked, "Lord, who is the one that's going to betray you?" ²¹ When Peter saw him, he said to Jesus, "Lord, what about him?"

²² "If I want him to remain until I come," Jesus answered, "what is that to you? As for you, follow me."

[23] So this rumor spread to the brothers and sisters that this disciple would not die. Yet Jesus did not tell him that he would not die, but, "If I want him to remain until I come, what is that to you?"

♥ GOING DEEPER

2 PETER 1:3–15

Growth in the Faith

[3] His divine power has given us everything required for life and godliness through the knowledge of him who called us by his own glory and goodness. [4] By these he has given us very great and precious promises, so that through them you may share in the divine nature, escaping the corruption that is in the world because of evil desire. [5] For this very reason, make every effort to supplement your faith with goodness, goodness with knowledge, [6] knowledge with self-control, self-control with endurance, endurance with godliness, [7] godliness with brotherly affection, and brotherly affection with love. [8] For if you possess these qualities in increasing measure, they will keep you from being useless or unfruitful in the knowledge of our Lord Jesus Christ. [9] The person who lacks these things is blind and shortsighted and has forgotten the cleansing from his past sins. [10] Therefore, brothers and sisters, make every effort to confirm your calling and election, because if you do these things you will never stumble. [11] For in this way, entry into the eternal kingdom of our Lord and Savior Jesus Christ will be richly provided for you.

[12] Therefore I will always remind you about these things, even though you know them and are established in the truth you now have. [13] I think it is right, as long as I am in this bodily tent, to wake you up with a reminder, [14] since I know that I will soon lay aside my tent, as our Lord Jesus Christ has indeed made clear to me. [15] And I will also make every effort so that you are able to recall these things at any time after my departure.

DATE: /   /

WHAT WAS PETER'S RESPONSE TO THE RESURRECTED CHRIST?

HOW CAN I RESPOND TO CHRIST BY DEMONSTRATING LOVE FOR THE LORD AND HIS PEOPLE?

Jesus's Ascension into Heaven

...he was taken up as they were watching...

ACTS 1:9

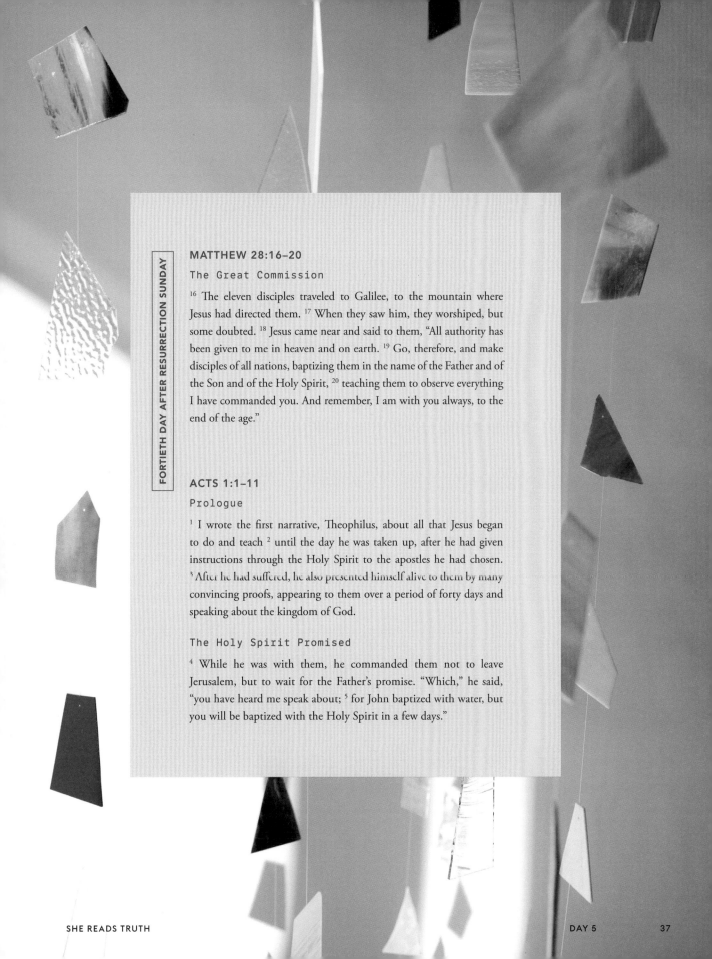

MATTHEW 28:16–20

The Great Commission

[16] The eleven disciples traveled to Galilee, to the mountain where Jesus had directed them. [17] When they saw him, they worshiped, but some doubted. [18] Jesus came near and said to them, "All authority has been given to me in heaven and on earth. [19] Go, therefore, and make disciples of all nations, baptizing them in the name of the Father and of the Son and of the Holy Spirit, [20] teaching them to observe everything I have commanded you. And remember, I am with you always, to the end of the age."

ACTS 1:1–11

Prologue

[1] I wrote the first narrative, Theophilus, about all that Jesus began to do and teach [2] until the day he was taken up, after he had given instructions through the Holy Spirit to the apostles he had chosen. [3] After he had suffered, he also presented himself alive to them by many convincing proofs, appearing to them over a period of forty days and speaking about the kingdom of God.

The Holy Spirit Promised

[4] While he was with them, he commanded them not to leave Jerusalem, but to wait for the Father's promise. "Which," he said, "you have heard me speak about; [5] for John baptized with water, but you will be baptized with the Holy Spirit in a few days."

⁶ So when they had come together, they asked him, "Lord, are you restoring the kingdom to Israel at this time?"

⁷ He said to them, "It is not for you to know times or periods that the Father has set by his own authority. ⁸ But you will receive power when the Holy Spirit has come on you, and you will be my witnesses in Jerusalem, in all Judea and Samaria, and to the ends of the earth."

The Ascension

⁹ After he had said this, he was taken up as they were watching, and a cloud took him out of their sight. ¹⁰ While he was going, they were gazing into heaven, and suddenly two men in white clothes stood by them. ¹¹ They said, "Men of Galilee, why do you stand looking up into heaven? This same Jesus, who has been taken from you into heaven, will come in the same way that you have seen him going into heaven."

GOING DEEPER

DEUTERONOMY 31:6

Be strong and courageous; don't be terrified or afraid of them. For the LORD your God is the one who will go with you; he will not leave you or abandon you.

HEBREWS 7:26–27

²⁶ For this is the kind of high priest we need: holy, innocent, undefiled, separated from sinners, and exalted above the heavens. ²⁷ He doesn't need to offer sacrifices every day, as high priests do—first for their own sins, then for those of the people. He did this once for all time when he offered himself.

HEBREWS 10:11–14

¹¹ Every priest stands day after day ministering and offering the same sacrifices time after time, which can never take away sins.

¹² But this man, after offering one sacrifice for sins forever, sat down at the right hand of God.

¹³ He is now waiting until his enemies are made his footstool. ¹⁴ For by one offering he has perfected forever those who are sanctified.

DATE: /   /

WHERE IS JESUS NOW?

WHAT HAS JESUS INSTRUCTED ME TO DO WHILE I AWAIT HIS RETURN?

Create Your Own Floral Arrangement

SUPPLIES

Water

Fresh flowers

Flower food

Gloves

Vase
or container
of your choice

Scissors
or gardening
shears

Fresh
greenery
and fillers

OPTIONAL SUPPLIES: Floral tape and wire

DIRECTIONS

01/ After purchasing your flowers and greenery, remove from packaging as soon as possible to allow the flowers to relax and begin opening up.

02/ Add room temperature water to a vase. Stir in 1 tablespoon of flower food (or half a packet). Let it dissolve while you prepare the stems.

 HELPFUL TIP EUCALYPTUS IS OFTEN USED FOR GREENERY AND GIVES THE ARRANGEMENT A NICE AROMA.

03/ You may want to use scissors and gloves for this process. Starting with greenery, remove leaves and thorns from the bottom half of the stem. This keeps the water clean so the arrangement stays fresh longer. Repeat with flowers, keeping smaller leaves toward the top of the stem to fill in the arrangement.

04/ If you are working with roses, remove thorns, guard petals, and any other petals that seem to have visible bruising. Then hold the rose down and toward your feet, gently twist the stem between your hands to help fluff out the petals. Gently push from the bottom of the petal to pop it backwards in order to give it more dimension.

FLOWERS LIKE RANUNCULUS AND ANEMONE HAVE DAINTY STEMS AND NEED EXTRA FLORAL WIRE FOR REINFORCEMENT.

05/ Trim each stem at an angle, then sort each type of flower and greenery into separate piles.

06/ Select three pieces of greenery and one flower—this is the center of your arrangement. As you add in each piece, twist stems in your hand. Keep your hands loose, not gripping stems tightly.

07/ Assemble arrangement in your hands by adding in a variety of flowers and greenery, working from the center out. Add greenery as you add florals to each side.

08/ Pause to consider the dimension of your arrangement. Tuck some stems lower and others higher to accomplish your desired shape.

 AFTER A FEW DAYS, REPLACE OLD WATER AND TRIM STEMS AGAIN AT AN ANGLE TO MAKE THE ARRANGEMENT LAST LONGER.

09/ Once your arrangement is complete in your hands, place in vase. Make sure stems are cut to the right length so that the lowest bud sits just above the rim of the vase. Fill any holes in your arrangement with remaining flowers or greenery. You can use floral tape near the buds to keep the structure.

10/ If you are putting this together for an event, wait to assemble your piece until the day before or the morning the arrangement is needed. Store your finished arrangement in a cool room until you are ready to transport it for display.

Take this day to catch up on your reading,
pray, and rest in the presence of the Lord.

But he was pierced because of our rebellion, crushed because of our iniquities; punishment for our peace was on him, and we are healed by his wounds.

ISAIAH 53:5

Weekly Truth

Scripture is God-breathed and true.
When we memorize it, we carry the good
news of Jesus with us wherever we go.

This week we will work on memorizing
1 Peter 1:3, the first verse of our key
passage. This verse reminds us of the
new life believers are given through
Christ's resurrection.

1 PETER 1:3-4

<u>³ Blessed be the God and Father of our Lord Jesus</u>
<u>Christ. Because of his great mercy he has given</u>
<u>us new birth into a living hope through the</u>
<u>resurrection of Jesus Christ from the dead</u>
⁴ and into an inheritance that is imperishable,
undefiled, and unfading, kept in heaven for you.

SEE TIPS FOR MEMORIZING SCRIPTURE ON PAGE 116.

OUR RESURRECTED LIFE IN CHRIST

SECTION TWO

Weeks 2 and 3 will look at many passages throughout the New Testament that describe what Jesus's resurrection has accomplished for believers and how it changes our lives both now and for eternity.

SECTION TWO

Christ's Resurrection Guarantees Ours

...in Christ all will be made alive.

1 CORINTHIANS 15:22

1 CORINTHIANS 15:1-28

Resurrection Essential to the Gospel

[1] Now I want to make clear for you, brothers and sisters, the gospel I preached to you, which you received, on which you have taken your stand [2] and by which you are being saved, if you hold to the message I preached to you—unless you believed in vain. [3] For I passed on to you as most important what I also received: that Christ died for our sins according to the Scriptures, [4] that he was buried, that he was raised on the third day according to the Scriptures, [5] and that he appeared to Cephas, then to the Twelve. [6] Then he appeared to over five hundred brothers and sisters at one time; most of them are still alive, but some have fallen asleep. [7] Then he appeared to James, then to all the apostles. [8] Last of all, as to one born at the wrong time, he also appeared to me.

[9] For I am the least of the apostles, not worthy to be called an apostle, because I persecuted the church of God. [10] But by the grace of God I am what I am, and his grace toward me was not in vain. On the contrary, I worked harder than any of them, yet not I, but the grace of God that was with me. [11] Whether, then, it is I or they, so we proclaim and so you have believed.

Resurrection Essential to the Faith

[12] Now if Christ is proclaimed as raised from the dead, how can some of you say, "There is no resurrection of the dead"? [13] If there is no resurrection of the dead, then not even Christ has been raised; [14] and if Christ has not been raised, then our proclamation is in vain, and so is your faith. [15] Moreover, we are found to be false witnesses about God, because we have testified wrongly about God that he raised up Christ—whom he did not raise up, if in fact the dead are not raised. [16] For if the dead are not raised, not even Christ has been raised. [17] And if Christ has not been raised, your faith is worthless; you are still in your sins. [18] Those, then, who have fallen asleep in Christ have also perished. [19] If we have put our hope in Christ for this life only, we should be pitied more than anyone.

Christ's Resurrection Guarantees Ours

[20] But as it is,

Christ has been raised from the dead, the firstfruits of those who have fallen asleep.

[21] For since death came through a man, the resurrection of the dead also comes through a man. [22] For just as in Adam all die, so also in Christ all will be made alive.

[23] But each in his own order: Christ, the firstfruits; afterward, at his coming, those who belong to Christ. [24] Then comes the end, when he hands over the kingdom to God the Father, when he abolishes all rule and all authority and power. [25] For he must reign until he puts all his enemies under his feet. [26] The last enemy to be abolished is death. [27] For God has put everything under his feet. Now when it says "everything" is put under him, it is obvious that he who puts everything under him is the exception. [28] When everything is subject to Christ, then the Son himself will also be subject to the one who subjected everything to him, so that God may be all in all.

ROMANS 5:12-21

Death Through Adam and Life Through Christ

[12] Therefore, just as sin entered the world through one man, and death through sin, in this way death spread to all people, because all sinned. [13] In fact, sin was in the world before the

law, but sin is not charged to a person's account when there is no law. ¹⁴ Nevertheless, death reigned from Adam to Moses, even over those who did not sin in the likeness of Adam's transgression. He is a type of the Coming One.

¹⁵ But the gift is not like the trespass. For if by the one man's trespass the many died, how much more have the grace of God and the gift which comes through the grace of the one man Jesus Christ overflowed to the many. ¹⁶ And the gift is not like the one man's sin, because from one sin came the judgment, resulting in condemnation, but from many trespasses came the gift, resulting in justification. ¹⁷ If by the one man's trespass, death reigned through that one man, how much more will those who receive the overflow of grace and the gift of righteousness reign in life through the one man, Jesus Christ.

¹⁸ So then, as through one trespass there is condemnation for everyone, so also through one righteous act there is justification leading to life for everyone. ¹⁹ For just as through one man's disobedience the many were made sinners, so also through the one man's obedience the many will be made righteous. ²⁰ The law came along to multiply the trespass. But where sin multiplied, grace multiplied even more ²¹ so that, just as sin reigned in death, so also grace will reign through righteousness, resulting in eternal life through Jesus Christ our Lord.

🛡 GOING DEEPER

GENESIS 3:1–7, 17–19

The Temptation and the Fall

¹ Now the serpent was the most cunning of all the wild animals that the LORD God had made. He said to the woman, "Did God really say, 'You can't eat from any tree in the garden'?"

² The woman said to the serpent, "We may eat the fruit from the trees in the garden. ³ But about the fruit of the tree in the middle of the garden, God said, 'You must not eat it or touch it, or you will die.'"

⁴ "No! You will certainly not die," the serpent said to the woman. ⁵ "In fact, God knows that when you eat it your eyes will be opened and you will be like God, knowing good and evil." ⁶ The woman saw that the tree was good for food and delightful to look at, and that it was desirable for obtaining wisdom. So she took some of its fruit and ate it; she also gave some to her husband, who was with her, and he ate it. ⁷ Then the eyes of both of them were opened, and they knew they were naked; so they sewed fig leaves together and made coverings for themselves.

…

¹⁷ And he said to the man, "Because you listened to your wife and ate from the tree about which I commanded you, 'Do not eat from it':

The ground is cursed because of you.
You will eat from it by means of painful labor
all the days of your life.
¹⁸ It will produce thorns and thistles for you,
and you will eat the plants of the field.
¹⁹ You will eat bread by the sweat of your brow
until you return to the ground,
since you were taken from it.
For you are dust,
and you will return to dust."

DATE: /   /

WHY IS THE RESURRECTION IMPORTANT TO MY FAITH?

WHAT BRINGS ME HOPE IN TODAY'S READING? WHAT CHALLENGES ME TO
LIVE DIFFERENTLY?

From Death to Life

But God, who is rich in
mercy, because of his great
love that he had for us, made
us alive with Christ...

EPHESIANS 2:4–5

EPHESIANS 2:1–10

From Death to Life

[1] And you were dead in your trespasses and sins [2] in which you previously walked according to the ways of this world, according to the ruler of the power of the air, the spirit now working in the disobedient. [3] We too all previously lived among them in our fleshly desires, carrying out the inclinations of our flesh and thoughts, and we were by nature children under wrath as the others were also. [4] But God, who is rich in mercy, because of his great love that he had for us, [5] made us alive with Christ even though we were dead in trespasses. You are saved by grace! [6] He also raised us up with him and seated us with him in the heavens in Christ Jesus, [7] so that in the coming ages he might display the immeasurable riches of his grace through his kindness to us in Christ Jesus. [8] For you are saved by grace through faith, and this is not from yourselves; it is God's gift— [9] not from works, so that no one can boast. [10] For we are his workmanship, created in Christ Jesus for good works, which God prepared ahead of time for us to do.

COLOSSIANS 1:13–14, 21–22

13 He has rescued us from the domain of darkness and transferred us into the kingdom of the Son he loves. 14 In him we have redemption, the forgiveness of sins.

…

21 Once you were alienated and hostile in your minds as expressed in your evil actions. 22 But now he has reconciled you by his physical body through his death, to present you holy, faultless, and blameless before him…

2 CORINTHIANS 5:16–21

The Ministry of Reconciliation

16 From now on, then, we do not know anyone from a worldly perspective. Even if we have known Christ from a worldly perspective, yet now we no longer know him in this way. 17 Therefore, if anyone is in Christ, he is a new creation; the old has passed away, and see, the new has come! 18 Everything is from God, who has reconciled us to himself through Christ and has given us the ministry of reconciliation. 19 That is, in Christ, God was reconciling the world to himself, not counting their trespasses against them, and he has committed the message of reconciliation to us.

20 Therefore, we are ambassadors for Christ, since God is making his appeal through us. We plead on Christ's behalf, "Be reconciled to God." 21 He made the one who did not know sin to be sin for us, so that in him we might become the righteousness of God.

♥ GOING DEEPER

PSALM 103:8–12

8 The LORD is compassionate and gracious,
slow to anger and abounding in faithful love.

9 He will not always accuse us
or be angry forever.
10 He has not dealt with us as our sins deserve
or repaid us according to our iniquities.

11 For as high as the heavens are above the earth,
so great is his faithful love
toward those who fear him.
12 As far as the east is from the west,
so far has he removed
our transgressions from us.

1 JOHN 4:9–10

9 God's love was revealed among us in this way:

God sent his one and only Son
into the world so that we might
live through him.

10 Love consists in this: not that we loved God, but that he loved us and sent his Son to be the atoning sacrifice for our sins.

HEBREWS 10:19–22

Exhortations to Godliness

19 Therefore, brothers and sisters, since we have boldness to enter the sanctuary through the blood of Jesus— 20 he has inaugurated for us a new and living way through the curtain (that is, through his flesh)— 21 and since we have a great high priest over the house of God, 22 let us draw near with a true heart in full assurance of faith, with our hearts sprinkled clean from an evil conscience and our bodies washed in pure water.

DATE: / /

HOW WOULD I DESCRIBE CHRIST'S FORGIVENESS OF MY SINS AFTER
TODAY'S READING?

WHAT BRINGS ME HOPE IN TODAY'S READING? WHAT CHALLENGES ME TO
LIVE DIFFERENTLY?

SECTION TWO

New Life in Christ

...Christ was raised from the dead by the glory of the Father, so we too may walk in newness of life.

ROMANS 6:4

ROMANS 6

The New Life in Christ

[1] What should we say then? Should we continue in sin so that grace may multiply? [2] Absolutely not! How can we who died to sin still live in it? [3] Or are you unaware that all of us who were baptized into Christ Jesus were baptized into his death? [4] Therefore we were buried with him by baptism into death, in order that, just as Christ was raised from the dead by the glory of the Father, so we too may walk in newness of life. [5] For if we have been united with him in the likeness of his death, we will certainly also be in the likeness of his resurrection. [6] For we know that our old self was crucified with him so that the body ruled by sin might be rendered powerless so that we may no longer be enslaved to sin, [7] since a person who has died is freed from sin. [8] Now if we died with Christ, we believe that we will also live with him, [9] because we know that Christ, having been raised from the dead, will not die again. Death no longer rules over him. [10] For the death he died, he died to sin once for all time; but the life he lives, he lives to God. [11] So, you too consider yourselves dead to sin and alive to God in Christ Jesus.

[12] Therefore do not let sin reign in your mortal body, so that you obey its desires. [13] And do not offer any parts of it to sin as weapons for unrighteousness. But as those who are alive from the dead, offer yourselves to God, and all the parts of yourselves to God as weapons for righteousness. [14] For sin will not rule over you, because you are not under the law but under grace.

From Slaves of Sin to Slaves of God

[15] What then? Should we sin because we are not under the law but under grace? Absolutely not! [16] Don't you know that if you offer yourselves to someone as obedient slaves, you are slaves of that one you obey—either of sin leading to death or of obedience leading to righteousness? [17] But thank God that, although you used to be slaves of sin, you obeyed from the heart that pattern of teaching to which you were handed over, [18] and having been set free from sin, you became enslaved to righteousness. [19] I am using a human analogy because of the weakness of your flesh. For just as you offered the parts of yourselves as slaves to impurity, and to greater and greater lawlessness, so now offer them as slaves to righteousness, which results in sanctification. [20] For when you were slaves of sin, you were free with regard to righteousness. [21] So what fruit was produced then from the things you are now ashamed of? The outcome of those things is death. [22] But now, since you have been set free from sin and have become enslaved to God, you have your fruit, which results in sanctification—and the outcome is eternal life! [23] For the wages of sin is death, but the gift of God is eternal life in Christ Jesus our Lord.

GALATIANS 2:20–21

[20] I have been crucified with Christ, and I no longer live, but Christ lives in me. The life I now live in the body, I live by faith in the Son of God, who loved me and gave himself for me. [21] I do not set aside the grace of God, for if righteousness comes through the law, then Christ died for nothing.

◗ GOING DEEPER

EZEKIEL 36:25–27

[25] "I will also sprinkle clean water on you, and you will be clean. I will cleanse you from all your impurities and all your idols. [26] I will give you a new heart and put a new spirit within you; I will remove your heart of stone and give you a heart of flesh. [27] I will place my Spirit within you and cause you to follow my statutes and carefully observe my ordinances."

1 PETER 2:24–25

[24] He himself bore our sins in his body on the tree; so that, having died to sins,

we might live for righteousness.

By his wounds you have been healed. [25] For you were like sheep going astray, but you have now returned to the Shepherd and Overseer of your souls.

GALATIANS 3:27

For those of you who were baptized into Christ have been clothed with Christ.

DATE: /   /

ACCORDING TO TODAY'S READING, HOW WOULD I DESCRIBE THE NEW LIFE IN CHRIST
I HAVE BEEN CALLED TO?

WHAT BRINGS ME HOPE IN TODAY'S READING? WHAT CHALLENGES ME TO
LIVE DIFFERENTLY?

Assurances of the Gospel

NEW LIFE IN CHRIST BEGINS WITH SALVATION. THE NEW TESTAMENT BUILDS ON THIS TRUTH, ASSURING BELIEVERS OF THE RESURRECTED LIFE THEY ARE GIVEN IN CHRIST. THESE WORDS OF CONFIDENCE FOUND IN SCRIPTURE REMIND BELIEVERS OF WHO THEY ARE AND WHAT THEY KNOW AS FOLLOWERS OF CHRIST. LISTED BELOW ARE TWENTY-NINE OF THESE ASSURANCES.

MT 7:21

Believers know the one who does the will of God will enter heaven.

MT 11:27

Believers know the Father because the Son has revealed Him.

JN 3:36

Believers know they have eternal life because of the Son.

JN 5:24

Believers know they have passed from death into life.

JN 10:10

Believers know they have abundant life.

JN 16:13

Believers know the truth because they have the Holy Spirit.

JN 17:21-23

Believers know they have fellowship with the Father, the Son, and the community of believers.

AC 1:8

Believers know they are empowered by the Holy Spirit to proclaim the good news of Jesus.

RM 5:5

Believers know God's love has been poured out in their hearts through the Holy Spirit.

RM 6:6

Believers know they are no longer enslaved to sin because they have been crucified with Christ.

RM 8:37-39

Believers know nothing can separate them from God's love.

1CO 3:16

Believers know that the Spirit of God dwells in them.

2CO 3:18

Believers know they are being transformed into the image of Christ.

GL 4:6

Believers know they are God's children and enjoy an intimate relationship with Him.

EXTRA

GL 5:16

Believers know the Holy
Spirit empowers them to
live lives free of sin.

EPH 6:11–18

Believers know they are
equipped with the armor
of God to resist the
powers of darkness.

PHP 3:9

Believers know their
righteousness is found
in Christ.

PHP 3:20

Believers know
their citizenship is
in heaven.

COL 3:4

Believers know Christ
is their life.

1TH 1:10

Believers know they
have been rescued from
God's coming wrath.

HEB 4:14–16

Believers know they
have neverending access
to God's presence.

HEB 12:5–7

Believers know
God disciplines them
because He loves
His children.

1PT 1:3–4

Believers know they
have an inheritance
reserved in heaven
for them.

1PT 1:18–19

Believers know Christ
paid for the redemption
of their sins with His
own blood.

2PT 1:3

Believers know God
has given them
everything required
for life and godliness.

1JN 2:1

Believers know Christ
is their advocate in the
face of sin.

1JN 5:1–5

Believers know that
by faith they have
been born of God and
that they have overcome
the world.

1JN 5:13–15

Believers know God
will hear anything
they ask of Him and
He will answer according
to His will.

RV 21–22

Believers know that at
Jesus's return, He will
create a new heaven and
a new earth, and God
will dwell with His
people forever.

The Gift of the Holy Spirit

...the law of the Spirit of
life in Christ Jesus has set
you free from the law of sin
and death.

ROMANS 8:2

ROMANS 8:1–4

The Life-Giving Spirit

¹ Therefore, there is now no condemnation for those in Christ Jesus, ² because the law of the Spirit of life in Christ Jesus has set you free from the law of sin and death. ³ For what the law could not do since it was weakened by the flesh, God did. He condemned sin in the flesh by sending his own Son in the likeness of sinful flesh as a sin offering, ⁴ in order that the law's requirement would be fulfilled in us who do not walk according to the flesh but according to the Spirit.

JOHN 14:15–20, 25–26

Another Counselor Promised

¹⁵ "If you love me, you will keep my commands. ¹⁶ And I will ask the Father, and he will give you another Counselor to be with you forever. ¹⁷ He is the Spirit of truth. The world is unable to receive him because it doesn't see him or know him. But you do know him, because he remains with you and will be in you.

The Father, the Son, and the Holy Spirit

[18] "I will not leave you as orphans; I am coming to you. [19] In a little while the world will no longer see me, but you will see me. Because I live, you will live too. [20] On that day you will know that I am in my Father, you are in me, and I am in you."

…

[25] "I have spoken these things to you while I remain with you. [26] But the Counselor, the Holy Spirit, whom the Father will send in my name, will teach you all things and remind you of everything I have told you."

JOHN 16:1–15

[1] "I have told you these things to keep you from stumbling. [2] They will ban you from the synagogues. In fact, a time is coming when anyone who kills you will think he is offering service to God. [3] They will do these things because they haven't known the Father or me. [4] But I have told you these things so that when their time comes you will remember I told them to you. I didn't tell you these things from the beginning, because I was with you. [5] But now I am going away to him who sent me, and not one of you asks me, 'Where are you going?' [6] Yet, because I have spoken these things to you, sorrow has filled your heart. [7] Nevertheless, I am telling you the truth. It is for your benefit that I go away, because if I don't go away the Counselor will not come to you. If I go, I will send him to you. [8] When he comes, he will convict the world about sin, righteousness, and judgment: [9] About sin, because they do not believe in me; [10] about righteousness, because I am going to the Father and you will no longer see me; [11] and about judgment, because the ruler of this world has been judged.

[12] "I still have many things to tell you, but you can't bear them now. [13] When the Spirit of truth comes, he will guide you into all the truth. For he will not speak on his own, but he will speak whatever he hears. He will also declare to you what is to come. [14] He will glorify me, because he will take from what is mine and declare it to you. [15] Everything the Father has is mine. This is why I told you that he takes from what is mine and will declare it to you."

TITUS 3:6–7

[6] He poured out his Spirit on us abundantly through Jesus Christ our Savior [7] so that, having been justified by his grace,

we may become heirs with the hope of eternal life.

1 JOHN 4:13–15

[13] This is how we know that we remain in him and he in us: He has given us of his Spirit. [14] And we have seen and we testify that the Father has sent his Son as the world's Savior. [15] Whoever confesses that Jesus is the Son of God—God remains in him and he in God.

◗ GOING DEEPER

JOEL 2:28–29

God's Promise of His Spirit

[28] "After this
I will pour out my Spirit on all humanity;
then your sons and your daughters will prophesy,
your old men will have dreams,
and your young men will see visions.
[29] I will even pour out my Spirit
on the male and female slaves in those days."

EPHESIANS 1:13–14

[13] In him you also were sealed with the promised Holy Spirit when you heard the word of truth, the gospel of your salvation, and when you believed. [14] The Holy Spirit is the down payment of our inheritance, until the redemption of the possession, to the praise of his glory.

DATE: /   /

HOW WOULD I DESCRIBE THE ROLE OF THE HOLY SPIRIT BASED ON TODAY'S READING?

WHAT BRINGS ME HOPE IN TODAY'S READING? WHAT CHALLENGES ME TO
LIVE DIFFERENTLY?

Walk by the Spirit

If we live by the Spirit, let us
also keep in step with the Spirit.

GALATIANS 5:25

GALATIANS 5

Freedom of the Christian

¹ For freedom, Christ set us free. Stand firm, then, and don't submit again to a yoke of slavery. ² Take note! I, Paul, am telling you that if you get yourselves circumcised, Christ will not benefit you at all. ³ Again I testify to every man who gets himself circumcised that he is obligated to do the entire law. ⁴ You who are trying to be justified by the law are alienated from Christ; you have fallen from grace. ⁵ For we eagerly await through the Spirit, by faith, the hope of righteousness. ⁶ For in Christ Jesus neither circumcision nor uncircumcision accomplishes anything; what matters is faith working through love.

⁷ You were running well. Who prevented you from being persuaded regarding the truth? ⁸ This persuasion does not come from the one who calls you. ⁹ A little leaven leavens the whole batch of dough. ¹⁰ I myself am persuaded in the Lord you will not accept any other view. But whoever it is that is confusing you will pay the penalty. ¹¹ Now brothers and sisters, if I still preach circumcision, why am I still persecuted? In that case the offense of the cross has been abolished. ¹² I wish those who are disturbing you might also let themselves be mutilated!

¹³ For you were called to be free, brothers and sisters; only don't use this freedom as an opportunity for the flesh, but serve one another through love. ¹⁴ For the whole law is fulfilled in one statement: Love your neighbor as yourself. ¹⁵ But if you bite and devour one another, watch out, or you will be consumed by one another.

The Spirit Versus the Flesh

¹⁶ I say, then, walk by the Spirit and you will certainly not carry out the desire of the flesh. ¹⁷ For the flesh desires what is against the Spirit, and the Spirit desires what is against the flesh; these are opposed to each other, so that you don't do what you want. ¹⁸ But if you are led by the Spirit, you are not under the law.

¹⁹ Now the works of the flesh are obvious: sexual immorality, moral impurity, promiscuity, ²⁰ idolatry, sorcery, hatreds, strife, jealousy, outbursts of anger, selfish ambitions, dissensions, factions, ²¹ envy, drunkenness, carousing, and anything similar. I am warning you about these things—as I warned you before—that those who practice such things will not inherit the kingdom of God.

²² But the fruit of the Spirit is love, joy, peace, patience, kindness, goodness, faithfulness, ²³ gentleness, and self-control. The law is not against such things. ²⁴ Now those who belong to Christ Jesus have crucified the flesh with its passions and desires. ²⁵ If we live by the Spirit, let us also keep in step with the Spirit. ²⁶ Let us not become conceited, provoking one another, envying one another.

ROMANS 8:5–17

⁵ For those who live according to the flesh have their minds set on the things of the flesh, but those who live according to the Spirit have their minds set on the things of the Spirit. ⁶ Now the mindset of the flesh is death, but the mindset of the Spirit is life and peace. ⁷ The mindset of the flesh is hostile to God because it does not submit to God's law. Indeed, it is unable to do so. ⁸ Those who are in the flesh cannot please God. ⁹ You, however, are not in the flesh, but in the Spirit, if indeed the Spirit of God lives in you. If anyone does not have the Spirit of Christ, he does not belong to him. ¹⁰ Now if Christ is in you, the body is dead because of sin, but the Spirit gives life because of righteousness. ¹¹ And if the Spirit of him who raised Jesus from the dead lives in you, then he who raised Christ from the dead will also bring your mortal bodies to life through his Spirit who lives in you.

The Holy Spirit's Ministries

¹² So then, brothers and sisters, we are not obligated to the flesh to live according to the flesh, ¹³ because if you live according to the flesh, you are going to die. But if by the Spirit you put to death the deeds of the body, you will live. ¹⁴ For all those led by God's Spirit are God's sons. ¹⁵ For you did not receive a spirit of slavery to fall back into fear.

Instead, you received the Spirit of adoption, by whom we cry out, "*Abba*, Father!" [16] The Spirit himself testifies together with our spirit that we are God's children, [17] and if children, also heirs—heirs of God and coheirs with Christ—if indeed we suffer with him so that we may also be glorified with him.

❤ GOING DEEPER

MICAH 6:8

Mankind, he has told each of you what is good
and what it is the Lord requires of you:
to act justly,
to love faithfulness,
and to walk humbly with your God.

1 CORINTHIANS 12:1–11
Diversity of Spiritual Gifts

[1] Now concerning spiritual gifts: brothers and sisters, I do not want you to be unaware. [2] You know that when you were pagans, you used to be enticed and led astray by mute idols. [3] Therefore I want you to know that no one speaking by the Spirit of God says, "Jesus is cursed," and no one can say, "Jesus is Lord," except by the Holy Spirit.

[4] Now there are different gifts, but the same Spirit. [5] There are different ministries, but the same Lord. [6] And there are different activities, but the same God works all of them in each person. [7] A manifestation of the Spirit is given to each person for the common good: [8] to one is given a message of wisdom through the Spirit, to another, a message of knowledge by the same Spirit, [9] to another, faith by the same Spirit, to another, gifts of healing by the one Spirit, [10] to another, the performing of miracles, to another, prophecy, to another, distinguishing between spirits, to another, different kinds of tongues, to another, interpretation of tongues. [11] One and the same Spirit is active in all these, distributing to each person as he wills.

DATE: / /

HOW ARE THE WORKS OF THE FLESH DIFFERENT FROM THE FRUIT OF THE SPIRIT?

WHAT BRINGS ME HOPE IN TODAY'S READING? WHAT CHALLENGES ME TO
LIVE DIFFERENTLY?

"

Our task in the present...is to live as
resurrection people....

N. T. WRIGHT

Take this day to catch up on your reading,
pray, and rest in the presence of the Lord.

"I will give you a new heart and put a new spirit within you; I will remove your heart of stone and give you a heart of flesh."

EZEKIEL 36:26

Weekly Truth

Scripture is God-breathed and true. When we memorize it, we carry the good news of Jesus with us wherever we go.

This week we will continue to memorize our key passage by adding verse 4. This verse is an encouragement of what is to come for believers.

1 PETER 1:3-4

³ Blessed be the God and Father of our Lord Jesus Christ. Because of his great mercy he has given us new birth into a living hope through the resurrection of Jesus Christ from the dead ⁴ and into an inheritance that is imperishable, undefiled, and unfading, kept in heaven for you.

SEE TIPS FOR MEMORIZING SCRIPTURE ON PAGE 116.

Seek the Things Above

So if you have been raised with Christ,
seek the things above...

COLOSSIANS 3:1

COLOSSIANS 3:1–17

The Life of the New Man

[1] So if you have been raised with Christ, seek the things above, where Christ is, seated at the right hand of God. [2] Set your minds on things above, not on earthly things. [3] For you died, and your life is hidden with Christ in God. [4] When Christ, who is your life, appears, then you also will appear with him in glory.

[5] Therefore, put to death what belongs to your earthly nature: sexual immorality, impurity, lust, evil desire, and greed, which is idolatry. [6] Because of these, God's wrath is coming upon the disobedient, [7] and you once walked in these things when you were living in them. [8] But now, put away all the following: anger, wrath, malice, slander, and filthy language from your mouth. [9] Do not lie to one another, since you have put off the old self with its practices [10] and have put on the new self. You are being renewed in knowledge according to the image of your Creator. [11] In Christ there is not Greek and Jew, circumcision and uncircumcision, barbarian, Scythian, slave and free; but Christ is all and in all.

The Christian Life

[12] Therefore, as God's chosen ones, holy and dearly loved, put on compassion, kindness, humility, gentleness, and patience, [13] bearing with one another and forgiving one another if anyone has a grievance against another. Just as the Lord has forgiven you, so you are also to forgive. [14] Above all, put on love, which is the perfect bond of unity.

[15] And let the peace of Christ, to which you were also called in one body, rule your hearts. And be thankful. [16] Let the word of Christ dwell richly among you, in all wisdom teaching and admonishing one another through psalms, hymns, and spiritual songs, singing to God with gratitude in your hearts. [17] And whatever you do, in word or in deed, do everything in the name of the Lord Jesus, giving thanks to God the Father through him.

EPHESIANS 4:17–32

Living the New Life

[17] Therefore, I say this and testify in the Lord: You should no longer walk as the Gentiles do, in the futility of their thoughts. [18] They are darkened in their understanding, excluded from the life of God, because of the ignorance that is in them and because of the hardness of their hearts. [19] They became callous and gave themselves over to promiscuity for the practice of every kind of impurity with a desire for more and more.

[20] But that is not how you came to know Christ, [21] assuming you heard about him and were taught by him, as the truth is in Jesus, [22] to take off your former way of life, the old self that is corrupted by deceitful desires, [23] to be renewed in the spirit of your minds, [24] and to

put on the new self, the one created according to God's likeness in righteousness and purity of the truth.

[25] Therefore, putting away lying, speak the truth, each one to his neighbor, because we are members of one another. [26] Be angry and do not sin. Don't let the sun go down on your anger, [27] and don't give the devil an opportunity. [28] Let the thief no longer steal. Instead, he is to do honest work with his own hands, so that he has something to share with anyone in need. [29] No foul language should come from your mouth, but only what is good for building up someone in need, so that it gives grace to those who hear. [30] And don't grieve God's Holy Spirit. You were sealed by him for the day of redemption. [31] Let all bitterness, anger and wrath, shouting and slander be removed from you, along with all malice. [32] And be kind and compassionate to one another, forgiving one another, just as God also forgave you in Christ.

◗ GOING DEEPER

LEVITICUS 20:26

You are to be holy to me because I, the LORD, am holy, and I have set you apart from the nations to be mine.

PSALM 1

The Two Ways

[1] How happy is the one who does not
walk in the advice of the wicked
or stand in the pathway with sinners
or sit in the company of mockers!
[2] Instead, his delight is in the LORD's instruction,
and he meditates on it day and night.
[3] He is like a tree planted beside flowing streams
that bears its fruit in its season,
and its leaf does not wither.
Whatever he does prospers.

[4] The wicked are not like this;
instead, they are like chaff that the wind blows away.
[5] Therefore the wicked will not stand up in the judgment,
nor sinners in the assembly of the righteous.

[6] For the LORD watches over the way of the righteous,
but the way of the wicked leads to ruin.

DATE: /   /

HOW DOES SCRIPTURE DESCRIBE A LIFE THAT SEEKS THE THINGS ABOVE?

WHAT BRINGS ME HOPE IN TODAY'S READING? WHAT CHALLENGES ME TO
LIVE DIFFERENTLY?

SECTION TWO

The Upside-Down Kingdom

"...the Son of Man did not come to be served, but to serve,
and to give his life as a ransom for many."

MATTHEW 20:28

MATTHEW 5:1–20, 33–48

¹ When he saw the crowds, he went up on the mountain, and after he sat down, his disciples came to him. ² Then he began to teach them, saying:

The Beatitudes

³ "Blessed are the poor in spirit,
for the kingdom of heaven is theirs.
⁴ Blessed are those who mourn,
for they will be comforted.
⁵ Blessed are the humble,
for they will inherit the earth.
⁶ Blessed are those who hunger and thirst for righteousness,
for they will be filled.
⁷ Blessed are the merciful,
for they will be shown mercy.
⁸ Blessed are the pure in heart,
for they will see God.
⁹ Blessed are the peacemakers,
for they will be called sons of God.
¹⁰ Blessed are those who are persecuted because
of righteousness,
for the kingdom of heaven is theirs.

¹¹ "You are blessed when they insult you and persecute you and falsely say every kind of evil against you because of me. ¹² Be glad and rejoice, because your reward is great in heaven. For that is how they persecuted the prophets who were before you.

Believers Are Salt and Light

¹³ "You are the salt of the earth. But if the salt should lose its taste, how can it be made salty? It's no longer good for anything but to be thrown out and trampled under people's feet.

¹⁴ "You are the light of the world. A city situated on a hill cannot be hidden. ¹⁵ No one lights a lamp and puts it under a basket, but rather on a lampstand, and it gives light for all who are in the house. ¹⁶ In the same way, let your light shine before others, so that they may see your good works and give glory to your Father in heaven.

Christ Fulfills the Law

¹⁷ "Don't think that I came to abolish the Law or the Prophets. I did not come to abolish but to fulfill. ¹⁸ For truly I tell you, until heaven and earth pass away, not the smallest letter or one stroke of a letter will pass away from the law until all things are accomplished. ¹⁹ Therefore, whoever breaks one of the least of these commands and teaches others to do the same will be called least in the kingdom of heaven. But whoever does and teaches these commands will be called great in the kingdom of heaven. ²⁰ For I tell you, unless your righteousness surpasses that of the scribes and Pharisees, you will never get into the kingdom of heaven."

. . .

Tell the Truth

³³ "Again, you have heard that it was said to our ancestors, You must not break your oath, but you must keep your oaths to the Lord. ³⁴ But I tell you, don't take an oath at all: either by heaven, because it is God's throne; ³⁵ or by the earth, because it is his footstool; or by Jerusalem, because it is the city of the great King. ³⁶ Do not swear by your head, because you cannot make a single hair white or black. ³⁷ But let your 'yes' mean 'yes,' and your 'no' mean 'no.' Anything more than this is from the evil one.

Go the Second Mile

³⁸ "You have heard that it was said, An eye for an eye and a tooth for a tooth. ³⁹ But I tell you, don't resist an evildoer. On the contrary, if anyone slaps you on your right cheek, turn the other to him also. ⁴⁰ As for the one who wants to sue you and take away your shirt, let him have your coat as well. ⁴¹ And if anyone forces you to go one mile, go with him two.

[42] Give to the one who asks you, and don't turn away from the one who wants to borrow from you.

Love Your Enemies

[43] "You have heard that it was said, Love your neighbor and hate your enemy. [44] But I tell you, love your enemies and pray for those who persecute you, [45] so that you may be children of your Father in heaven. For he causes his sun to rise on the evil and the good, and sends rain on the righteous and the unrighteous. [46] For if you love those who love you, what reward will you have? Don't even the tax collectors do the same? [47] And if you greet only your brothers and sisters, what are you doing out of the ordinary? Don't even the Gentiles do the same? [48] Be perfect, therefore, as your heavenly Father is perfect."

MATTHEW 20:26–28

[26] "It must not be like that among you. On the contrary, whoever wants to become great among you must be your servant, [27] and whoever wants to be first among you must be your slave; [28] just as the Son of Man did not come to be served, but to serve, and to give his life as a ransom for many."

PHILIPPIANS 2:3–8

[3] Do nothing out of selfish ambition or conceit, but in humility consider others as more important than yourselves. [4] Everyone should look not to his own interests, but rather to the interests of others.

Christ's Humility and Exaltation

[5] Adopt the same attitude as that of Christ Jesus,

[6] who, existing in the form of God,
did not consider equality with God
as something to be exploited.
[7] Instead he emptied himself
by assuming the form of a servant,
taking on the likeness of humanity.
And when he had come as a man,
[8] he humbled himself by becoming obedient
to the point of death—
even to death on a cross.

◆ GOING DEEPER

PSALM 15

A Description of the Godly

A psalm of David.

[1] Lord, who can dwell in your tent?
Who can live on your holy mountain?

[2] The one who lives blamelessly, practices righteousness,
and acknowledges the truth in his heart—
[3] who does not slander with his tongue,
who does not harm his friend
or discredit his neighbor,
[4] who despises the one rejected by the Lord
but honors those who fear the Lord,
who keeps his word whatever the cost,
[5] who does not lend his silver at interest
or take a bribe against the innocent—
the one who does these things will never be shaken.

DATE: /   /

HOW DO THE TEACHINGS OF JESUS IN TODAY'S READING DIFFER FROM THE WAYS OF THE WORLD?

WHAT BRINGS ME HOPE IN TODAY'S READING? WHAT CHALLENGES ME TO LIVE DIFFERENTLY?

"

A LIVING HOPE

In the end, his will, not ours, is done.
Love is the victor. Death is not the end.
The end is life. His life and our lives
through him, in him.

FREDERICK BUECHNER

Our Future Hope

"If I go away and prepare a
place for you, I will come again
and take you to myself, so that
where I am you may be also."

JOHN 14:3

JOHN 14:1-6

The Way to the Father

¹ "Don't let your heart be troubled. Believe in God; believe also in me. ² In my Father's house are many rooms. If it were not so, would I have told you that I am going to prepare a place for you? ³ If I go away and prepare a place for you, I will come again and take you to myself, so that where I am you may be also. ⁴ You know the way to where I am going."

⁵ "Lord," Thomas said, "we don't know where you're going. How can we know the way?"

⁶ Jesus told him, "I am the way, the truth, and the life. No one comes to the Father except through me."

1 THESSALONIANS 4:13-18

The Comfort of Christ's Coming

¹³ We do not want you to be uninformed, brothers and sisters, concerning those who are asleep, so that you will not grieve like the rest, who have no hope. ¹⁴ For if we believe that Jesus died and rose again, in the same

way, through Jesus, God will bring with him those who have fallen asleep. [15] For we say this to you by a word from the Lord: We who are still alive at the Lord's coming will certainly not precede those who have fallen asleep. [16] For the Lord himself will descend from heaven with a shout, with the archangel's voice, and with the trumpet of God, and the dead in Christ will rise first. [17] Then we who are still alive, who are left, will be caught up together with them in the clouds to meet the Lord in the air, and so we will always be with the Lord. [18] Therefore encourage one another with these words.

2 CORINTHIANS 4:7–18

Treasure in Clay Jars

[7] Now we have this treasure in clay jars, so that this extraordinary power may be from God and not from us. [8] We are afflicted in every way but not crushed; we are perplexed but not in despair; [9] we are persecuted but not abandoned; we are struck down but not destroyed. [10] We always carry the death of Jesus in our body, so that the life of Jesus may also be displayed in our body. [11] For we who live are always being given over to death for Jesus's sake, so that Jesus's life may also be displayed in our mortal flesh. [12] So then, death is at work in us, but life in you. [13] And since we have the same spirit of faith in keeping with what is written, I believed, therefore I spoke, we also believe, and therefore speak. [14] For we know that

<u>the one who raised the Lord Jesus will also raise us with Jesus</u>

and present us with you. [15] Indeed, everything is for your benefit so that, as grace extends through more and more people, it may cause thanksgiving to increase to the glory of God.

[16] Therefore we do not give up. Even though our outer person is being destroyed, our inner person is being renewed day by day. [17] For our momentary light affliction is producing for us an absolutely incomparable eternal weight of glory. [18] So we do not focus on what is seen, but on what is unseen. For what is seen is temporary, but what is unseen is eternal.

🔖 GOING DEEPER

PROVERBS 14:32

The wicked one is thrown down by his own sin,
but the righteous one has a refuge in his death.

ECCLESIASTES 3:11

He has made everything appropriate in its time. He has also put eternity in their hearts, but no one can discover the work God has done from beginning to end.

DATE: /   /

HOW CAN THE PROMISE OF CHRIST'S RETURN SHAPE HOW I LIVE NOW?

WHAT BRINGS ME HOPE IN TODAY'S READING? WHAT CHALLENGES ME TO
LIVE DIFFERENTLY?

EXTRA

Hope Even in Death

Since Adam and Eve first sinned in the garden, death has been an enemy that overtakes each of us. Because we are living in a broken world, all of creation feels the weight and reality of death. But we are not without hope! Though death's power is great, God's power is greater still.

The following pages summarize some of what Scripture says about believers' hope in the face of death.

ONE

God has authority and power over life and death.

See now that I alone am he;
there is no God but me.
I bring death and I give life...
DT 32:39

The Lord brings death and gives life;
he sends some down to Sheol, and he raises others up.
1SM 2:6

For I am persuaded that neither death nor life, nor angels
nor rulers, nor things present nor things to come, nor
powers, nor height nor depth, nor any other created thing
will be able to separate us from the love of God that is in
Christ Jesus our Lord.
RM 8:38–39

TWO

God can bypass natural death and He can resurrect the dead.

Enoch walked with God; then he was not there because God
took him.
GN 5:24 (SEE HEB 11:5)

As they continued walking and talking, a chariot of fire with
horses of fire suddenly appeared and separated the two of
them. Then Elijah went up into heaven in the whirlwind.
2KG 2:11

So I prophesied as I had been commanded. While I was
prophesying, there was a noise, a rattling sound, and the
bones came together, bone to bone. As I looked, tendons
appeared on them, flesh grew, and skin covered them, but
there was no breath in them. He said to me, "Prophesy to the
breath, prophesy, son of man. Say to it: This is what the
Lord God says: Breath, come from the four winds and breathe
into these slain so that they may live!" So I prophesied as
he commanded me; the breath entered them, and they came to
life and stood on their feet, a vast army.
EZK 37:7–10

After he said this, he shouted with a loud voice, "Lazarus,
come out!" The dead man came out bound hand and foot with
linen strips and with his face wrapped in a cloth. Jesus
said to them, "Unwrap him and let him go."
JN 11:43–44

2/3

THREE

There is hope for both spiritual and bodily rescue from death.

But I know that my Redeemer lives,
and at the end he will stand on the dust.
Even after my skin has been destroyed,
yet I will see God in my flesh.
I will see him myself;
my eyes will look at him, and not as a stranger.
My heart longs within me.
JB 19:25–27

Your dead will live; their bodies will rise.
Awake and sing, you who dwell in the dust!
For you will be covered with the morning dew,
and the earth will bring out the departed spirits.
IS 26:19

Many who sleep in the dust
of the earth will awake,
some to eternal life,
and some to disgrace and eternal contempt.
DN 12:2

We do not want you to be uninformed, brothers and sisters,
concerning those who are asleep, so that you will not grieve
like the rest, who have no hope. For if we believe that Jesus
died and rose again, in the same way, through Jesus, God will
bring with him those who have fallen asleep.
1TH 4:13–14

By faith Abraham, when he was tested, offered up Isaac....
He considered God to be able even to raise someone from the
dead; therefore, he received him back, figuratively speaking.
HEB 11:17, 19 (SEE GN 22:1–15)

FOUR

Christ is the fulfillment and image of our resurrection hope.

The people who live in darkness
have seen a great light,
and for those living in the land
 of the shadow of death,
a light has dawned.
MT 4:16

Jesus said to her, "I am the resurrection and the life.
The one who believes in me, even if he dies, will live."
JN 11:25

God raised him up, ending the pains of death, because it was
not possible for him to be held by death.
AC 2:24

For if we have been united with him in the likeness of
his death, we will certainly also be in the likeness of
his resurrection.
RM 6:5

For the wages of sin is death, but the gift of God is
eternal life in Christ Jesus our Lord.
RM 6:23

If we have put our hope in Christ for this life only,
we should be pitied more than anyone.
1CO 15:19

For since death came through a man, the resurrection
of the dead also comes through a man.
1CO 15:21

But we do see Jesus—made lower than the angels for a
short time so that by God's grace he might taste death
for everyone—crowned with glory and honor because he
suffered death.
HEB 2:9

3/3

FIVE

Christ is with us in both life and death.

"This is eternal life: that they may know you, the only true God, and the one you have sent—Jesus Christ."
JN 17:3

We always carry the death of Jesus in our body, so that the life of Jesus may also be displayed in our body.
2CO 4:10

For me, to live is Christ and to die is gain.
PHP 1:21

SIX

Death will be defeated, once and for all.

The last enemy to be abolished is death.
1CO 15:26

When this corruptible body is clothed with incorruptibility, and this mortal body is clothed with immortality, then the saying that is written will take place:

> Death has been swallowed up in victory.
> Where, death, is your victory?
> Where, death, is your sting?

1CO 15:54–55

He will wipe away every tear from their eyes. Death will be no more; grief, crying, and pain will be no more, because the previous things have passed away.
RV 21:4

The Nature of the Resurrection Body

He will transform the body of
our humble condition into the
likeness of his glorious body...

PHILIPPIANS 3:21

1 CORINTHIANS 15:35–49

The Nature of the Resurrection Body

[35] But someone will ask, "How are the dead raised? What kind of body will they have when they come?" [36] You fool! What you sow does not come to life unless it dies. [37] And as for what you sow—you are not sowing the body that will be, but only a seed, perhaps of wheat or another grain. [38] But God gives it a body as he wants, and to each of the seeds its own body. [39] Not all flesh is the same flesh; there is one flesh for humans, another for animals, another for birds, and another for fish. [40] There are heavenly bodies and earthly bodies, but the splendor of the heavenly bodies is different from that of the earthly ones. [41] There is a splendor of the sun, another of the moon, and another of the stars; in fact, one star differs from another star in splendor. [42] So it is with the resurrection of the dead: Sown in corruption, raised in incorruption; [43] sown in dishonor, raised in glory; sown in weakness, raised in power; [44] sown a natural body, raised a spiritual body. If there is a natural body, there is also a spiritual body. [45] So it is written, The first man Adam became a living being; the last Adam became a life-giving spirit. [46] However, the spiritual is not first, but the natural, then the spiritual.

[47] The first man was from the earth, a man of dust; the second man is from heaven. [48] Like the man of dust, so are those who are of the dust; like the man of heaven, so are those who are of heaven. [49] And just as we have borne the image of the man of dust, we will also bear the image of the man of heaven.

2 CORINTHIANS 5:1-15

Our Future After Death

¹ For we know that if our earthly tent we live in is destroyed, we have a building from God, an eternal dwelling in the heavens, not made with hands. ² Indeed, we groan in this tent, desiring to put on our heavenly dwelling, ³ since, when we are clothed, we will not be found naked. ⁴ Indeed, we groan while we are in this tent, burdened as we are, because we do not want to be unclothed but clothed, so that mortality may be swallowed up by life. ⁵ Now the one who prepared us for this very purpose is God, who gave us the Spirit as a down payment.

⁶ So we are always confident and know that while we are at home in the body we are away from the Lord. ⁷ For we walk by faith, not by sight. ⁸ In fact, we are confident, and we would prefer to be away from the body and at home with the Lord. ⁹ Therefore, whether we are at home or away, we make it our aim to be pleasing to him. ¹⁰ For we must all appear before the judgment seat of Christ, so that each may be repaid for what he has done in the body, whether good or evil.

¹¹ Therefore, since we know the fear of the Lord, we try to persuade people. What we are is plain to God, and I hope it is also plain to your consciences. ¹² We are not commending ourselves to you again, but giving you an opportunity to be proud of us, so that you may have a reply for those who take pride in outward appearance rather than in the heart. ¹³ For if we are out of our mind, it is for God; if we are in our right mind, it is for you. ¹⁴ For the love of Christ compels us, since we have reached this conclusion, that one died for all, and therefore all died.

¹⁵ And he died for all so that those who live should no longer live for themselves, but for the one who died for them and was raised.

PHILIPPIANS 3:20-21

²⁰ Our citizenship is in heaven, and we eagerly wait for a Savior from there, the Lord Jesus Christ. ²¹ He will transform the body of our humble condition into the likeness of his glorious body, by the power that enables him to subject everything to himself.

♥ GOING DEEPER

JOB 19:25-27

²⁵ But I know that my Redeemer lives,
and at the end he will stand on the dust.
²⁶ Even after my skin has been destroyed,
yet I will see God in my flesh.
²⁷ I will see him myself;
my eyes will look at him, and not as a stranger.
My heart longs within me.

ISAIAH 26:19

Your dead will live; their bodies will rise.
Awake and sing, you who dwell in the dust!
For you will be covered with the morning dew,
and the earth will bring out the departed spirits.

1 CORINTHIANS 13:12

For now we see only a reflection as in a mirror, but then face to face. Now I know in part, but then I will know fully, as I am fully known.

DATE: /   /

WHAT DOES TODAY'S READING TELL ME ABOUT MY FUTURE AFTER DEATH?

WHAT BRINGS ME HOPE IN TODAY'S READING? WHAT CHALLENGES ME TO
LIVE DIFFERENTLY?

Our Eternal Victory

Where, death, is your victory?
Where, death, is your sting?

1 CORINTHIANS 15:55

1 CORINTHIANS 15:50–58

Victorious Resurrection

⁵⁰ What I am saying, brothers and sisters, is this: Flesh and blood cannot inherit the kingdom of God, nor can corruption inherit incorruption. ⁵¹ Listen, I am telling you a mystery: We will not all fall asleep, but we will all be changed, ⁵² in a moment, in the twinkling of an eye, at the last trumpet. For the trumpet will sound, and the dead will be raised incorruptible, and we will be changed. ⁵³ For this corruptible body must be clothed with incorruptibility, and this mortal body must be clothed with immortality. ⁵⁴ When this corruptible body is clothed with incorruptibility, and this mortal body is clothed with immortality, then the saying that is written will take place:

Death has been swallowed up in victory.
⁵⁵ Where, death, is your victory?
Where, death, is your sting?

⁵⁶ The sting of death is sin, and the power of sin is the law. ⁵⁷ But thanks be to God, who gives us the victory through our Lord Jesus Christ!

⁵⁸ Therefore, my dear brothers and sisters, be steadfast, immovable, always excelling in the Lord's work, because you know that your labor in the Lord is not in vain.

REVELATION 21

The New Creation

[1] Then I saw a new heaven and a new earth; for the first heaven and the first earth had passed away, and the sea was no more. [2] I also saw the holy city, the new Jerusalem, coming down out of heaven from God, prepared like a bride adorned for her husband.

[3] Then I heard a loud voice from the throne: Look, God's dwelling is with humanity, and he will live with them. They will be his peoples, and God himself will be with them and will be their God.

[4] He will wipe away every tear from their eyes. Death will be no more; grief, crying, and pain will be no more, because the previous things have passed away.

[5] Then the one seated on the throne said, "Look, I am making everything new." He also said, "Write, because these words are faithful and true." [6] Then he said to me, "It is done! I am the Alpha and the Omega, the beginning and the end. I will freely give to the thirsty from the spring of the water of life. [7] The one who conquers will inherit these things, and I will be his God, and he will be my son. [8] But the cowards, faithless, detestable, murderers, sexually immoral, sorcerers, idolaters, and all liars—their share will be in the lake that burns with fire and sulfur, which is the second death."

The New Jerusalem

[9] Then one of the seven angels, who had held the seven bowls filled with the seven last plagues, came and spoke with me: "Come, I will show you the bride, the wife of the Lamb." [10] He then carried me away in the Spirit to a great, high mountain and showed me the holy city, Jerusalem, coming down out of heaven from God, [11] arrayed with God's glory. Her radiance was like a precious jewel, like a jasper stone, clear as crystal. [12] The city had a massive high wall, with twelve gates. Twelve angels were at the gates; the names of the twelve tribes of Israel's sons were inscribed on the gates. [13] There were three gates on the east, three gates on the north, three gates on the south, and three gates on the west.

[14] The city wall had twelve foundations, and the twelve names of the twelve apostles of the Lamb were on the foundations.

[15] The one who spoke with me had a golden measuring rod to measure the city, its gates, and its wall. [16] The city is laid out in a square; its length and width are the same. He measured the city with the rod at 12,000 *stadia*. Its length, width, and height are equal. [17] Then he measured its wall, 144 cubits according to human measurement, which the angel used. [18] The building material of its wall was jasper, and the city was pure gold clear as glass. [19] The foundations of the city wall were adorned with every kind of jewel: the first foundation is jasper, the second sapphire, the third chalcedony, the fourth emerald, [20] the fifth sardonyx, the sixth carnelian, the seventh chrysolite, the eighth beryl, the ninth topaz, the tenth chrysoprase, the eleventh jacinth, the twelfth amethyst. [21] The twelve gates are twelve pearls; each individual gate was made of a single pearl. The main street of the city was pure gold, transparent as glass.

[22] I did not see a temple in it, because the Lord God the Almighty and the Lamb are its temple. [23] The city does not need the sun or the moon to shine on it, because the glory of God illuminates it, and its lamp is the Lamb. [24] The nations will walk by its light, and the kings of the earth will bring their glory into it. [25] Its gates will never close by day because it will never be night there. [26] They will bring the glory and honor of the nations into it. [27] Nothing unclean will ever enter it, nor anyone who does what is detestable or false, but only those written in the Lamb's book of life.

REVELATION 22

The Source of Life

[1] Then he showed me the river of the water of life, clear as crystal, flowing from the throne of God and of the Lamb [2] down the middle of the city's main street. The tree of life was on each side of the river, bearing twelve kinds of fruit, producing its fruit every month. The leaves of the tree are for healing the nations, [3] and there will no longer be any curse. The throne of God and of the Lamb will be in the city, and his servants will worship him. [4] They will see his face, and his name will be on their foreheads. [5] Night will be no more; people will not need the light of a lamp or the light of the sun, because the Lord God will give them light, and they will reign forever and ever.

NOTES

6 Then he said to me, "These words are faithful and true. The Lord, the God of the spirits of the prophets, has sent his angel to show his servants what must soon take place."

7 "Look, I am coming soon! Blessed is the one who keeps the words of the prophecy of this book."

8 I, John, am the one who heard and saw these things. When I heard and saw them, I fell down to worship at the feet of the angel who had shown them to me. 9 But he said to me, "Don't do that! I am a fellow servant with you, your brothers the prophets, and those who keep the words of this book. Worship God!"

10 Then he said to me, "Don't seal up the words of the prophecy of this book, because the time is near. 11 Let the unrighteous go on in unrighteousness; let the filthy still be filthy; let the righteous go on in righteousness; let the holy still be holy."

12 "Look, I am coming soon, and my reward is with me to repay each person according to his work. 13 I am the Alpha and the Omega, the first and the last, the beginning and the end.

14 "Blessed are those who wash their robes, so that they may have the right to the tree of life and may enter the city by the gates. 15 Outside are the dogs, the sorcerers, the sexually immoral, the murderers, the idolaters, and everyone who loves and practices falsehood.

16 "I, Jesus, have sent my angel to attest these things to you for the churches. I am the Root and descendant of David, the bright morning star."

17 Both the Spirit and the bride say, "Come!" Let anyone who hears, say, "Come!" Let the one who is thirsty come. Let the one who desires take the water of life freely.

18 I testify to everyone who hears the words of the prophecy of this book: If anyone adds to them, God will add to him the plagues that are written in this book. 19 And if anyone takes away from the words of the book of this prophecy, God will take away his share of the tree of life and the holy city, which are written about in this book.

20 He who testifies about these things says, "Yes, I am coming soon."

Amen! Come, Lord Jesus!

21 The grace of the Lord Jesus be with everyone. Amen.

🔖 GOING DEEPER

ISAIAH 25:8–9

8 When he has swallowed up death once and for all,
the Lord God will wipe away the tears
from every face
and remove his people's disgrace
from the whole earth,
for the LORD has spoken.

9 On that day it will be said,
"Look, this is our God;
we have waited for him, and he has saved us.
This is the LORD; we have waited for him.
Let's rejoice and be glad in his salvation."

DATE: /   /

WHAT DOES TODAY'S READING TELL ME ABOUT WHAT ETERNITY WILL BE LIKE?

WHAT BRINGS ME HOPE IN TODAY'S READING? WHAT CHALLENGES ME TO
LIVE DIFFERENTLY?

Hallelujah, We Shall Rise

1. In the re-sur-rect-ion morn-ing, When the trump of God shall sound, We shall
2. In the re-sur-rect-ion morn-ing, What a meet - ing it will be, We shall
3. In the re-sur-rect-ion morn-ing, Bless-èd thought it is to me, We shall
4. In the re-sur-rect-ion morn-ing, We shall meet Him in the air, We shall

rise, we shall rise! Then the saints will come re - joic-ing and no
rise, we shall rise! When our fa - thers and our mo - thers, And our
rise, we shall rise! I shall see my bless - èd Sav-ior, Who so
rise, we shall rise! And be car-ried up to glor-y, To our

tears will e'er be found, We shall rise, we shall rise.
loved ones we shall see, We shall rise, we shall rise!
free - ly died for me, We shall rise, we shall rise!
home so bright and fair, We shall rise, we shall rise!

WORDS & MUSIC
John Edmond Thomas, 1904

Take this day to catch up on your reading,
pray, and rest in the presence of the Lord.

I have been crucified with Christ, and I no longer live, but Christ lives in me. The life I now live in the body, I live by faith in the Son of God, who loved me and gave himself for me.

GALATIANS 2:20

Weekly Truth

Scripture is God-breathed and true. When we memorize it, we carry the good news of Jesus with us wherever we go.

For this plan we have worked to memorize our key passage, 1 Peter 1:3-4. Continue to repeat it as a reminder of the hope believers have in Christ's finished work and their future home.

1 PETER 1:3-4

³ Blessed be the God and Father of our Lord Jesus Christ. Because of his great mercy he has given us new birth into a living hope through the resurrection of Jesus Christ from the deadand into ⁴ an inheritance that is imperishable, undefiled, and unfading, kept in heaven for you.

SEE TIPS FOR MEMORIZING SCRIPTURE ON PAGE 116.

BENEDICTION

From "Resurrection,"
in *The Valley of Vision*

What more could be done
than thou hast done!
Thy death is my life,
thy resurrection my peace,
thy ascension my hope,
thy prayers my comfort.

Tips for Memorizing Scripture

At She Reads Truth, we believe Scripture memorization is an important discipline in your walk with God. Committing God's Truth to memory means He can minister to us—and we can minister to others—through His Word no matter where we are. As you approach the Weekly Truth passage in this book, try these memorization tips to see which techniques work best for you!

STUDY IT

Study the passage in its biblical context and ask yourself a few questions before you begin to memorize it: What does this passage say? What does it mean? How would I say this in my own words? What does it teach me about God? Understanding what the passage means helps you know why it is important to carry it with you wherever you go.

Break the passage into smaller sections, memorizing a phrase at a time.

PRAY IT

Use the passage you are memorizing as a prompt for prayer.

WRITE IT

Dedicate a notebook to Scripture memorization and write the passage over and over again.

Diagram the passage after you write it out. Place a square around the verbs, underline the nouns, and circle any adjectives or adverbs. Say the passage aloud several times, emphasizing the verbs as you repeat it. Then do the same thing again with the nouns, then the adjectives and adverbs.

Write out the first letter of each word in the passage somewhere you can reference it throughout the week as you work on your memorization.

Use a whiteboard to write out the passage. Erase a few words at a time as you continue to repeat it aloud. Keep erasing parts of the passage until you have it all committed to memory.

CREATE

If you can, make up a tune for the passage to sing as you go about your day, or try singing it to the tune of a favorite song.

Sketch the passage, visualizing what each phrase would look like in the form of a picture. Or, try using calligraphy or altering the style of your handwriting as you write it out.

Use hand signals or signs to come up with associations for each word or phrase and repeat the movements as you practice.

SAY IT

Repeat the passage out loud to yourself as you are going through the rhythm of your day—getting ready, pouring your coffee, waiting in traffic, or making dinner.

Listen to the passage read aloud to you.

Record a voice memo on your phone and listen to it throughout the day or play it on an audio Bible.

SHARE IT

Memorize the passage with a friend, family member, or mentor. Spontaneously challenge each other to recite the passage, or pick a time to review your passage and practice saying it from memory together.

Send the passage as an encouraging text to a friend, testing yourself as you type to see how much you have memorized so far.

KEEP AT IT!

Set reminders on your phone to prompt you to practice your passage.

Purchase a She Reads Truth 12 Card Set or keep a stack of note cards with Scripture you are memorizing by your bed. Practice reciting what you've memorized previously before you go to sleep, ending with the passages you are currently learning. If you wake up in the middle of the night, review them again instead of grabbing your phone. Read them out loud before you get out of bed in the morning.

CSB BOOK ABBREVIATIONS

OLD TESTAMENT

GN Genesis	**JB** Job	**HAB** Habakkuk	**PHP** Philippians
EX Exodus	**PS** Psalms	**ZPH** Zephaniah	**COL** Colossians
LV Leviticus	**PR** Proverbs	**HG** Haggai	**1TH** 1 Thessalonians
NM Numbers	**EC** Ecclesiastes	**ZCH** Zechariah	**2TH** 2 Thessalonians
DT Deuteronomy	**SG** Song of Solomon	**MAL** Malachi	**1TM** 1 Timothy
JOS Joshua	**IS** Isaiah		**2TM** 2 Timothy
JDG Judges	**JR** Jeremiah	NEW TESTAMENT	**TI** Titus
RU Ruth	**LM** Lamentations	**MT** Matthew	**PHM** Philemon
1SM 1 Samuel	**EZK** Ezekiel	**MK** Mark	**HEB** Hebrews
2SM 2 Samuel	**DN** Daniel	**LK** Luke	**JMS** James
1KG 1 Kings	**HS** Hosea	**JN** John	**1PT** 1 Peter
2KG 2 Kings	**JL** Joel	**AC** Acts	**2PT** 2 Peter
1CH 1 Chronicles	**AM** Amos	**RM** Romans	**1JN** 1 John
2CH 2 Chronicles	**OB** Obadiah	**1CO** 1 Corinthians	**2JN** 2 John
EZR Ezra	**JNH** Jonah	**2CO** 2 Corinthians	**3JN** 3 John
NEH Nehemiah	**MC** Micah	**GL** Galatians	**JD** Jude
EST Esther	**NAH** Nahum	**EPH** Ephesians	**RV** Revelation

BIBLIOGRAPHY

Buechner, Frederick. *The Magnificent Defeat.* United Kingdom: HarperCollins, 1985.

Wright, N. T. *Surprised By Hope: Rethinking Heaven, the Resurrection, and the Mission of the Church.* New York: HarperCollins, 2008.

The Valley of Vision. United Kingdom: Banner of Truth Trust, 2003.

LOOKING FOR DEVOTIONALS?

Download the **She Reads Truth app** to find devotionals that complement your daily Scripture reading. If you're stuck on a passage, hop into the community discussion to connect with other Shes who are reading God's Word right along with you.

You just spent 21 days in the Word of God!

MY FAVORITE DAY OF THIS READING PLAN:

HOW DID I FIND DELIGHT IN GOD'S WORD?

ONE THING I LEARNED ABOUT GOD:

WHAT WAS GOD DOING IN MY LIFE DURING THIS STUDY?

WHAT DID I LEARN THAT I WANT TO SHARE WITH SOMEONE ELSE?

A SPECIFIC SCRIPTURE THAT ENCOURAGED ME:

A SPECIFIC SCRIPTURE THAT CHALLENGED AND CONVICTED ME: